the amazing temperaments

how to accept yourself, understand others, and like them anyway

a study of the four personality types

BIG
DREAM
MINISTRIES

No part of The Amazing Temperaments, whether audio, video, or print, may be reproduced in any form without written permission from Big Dream Ministries, Inc. P.O. Box 324, 12460 Crabapple Road, Suite 202, Alpharetta, Georgia, 30004.

ISBN 13: 978-1932-199-54-3
ISBN 10: 1-932199-54-3

Cover design by Melissa Swanson
Cover image by Big Stock
Creative Team: Terry Behimer, Traci Martin, Pat Reinheimer

Unless otherwise identified, all Scripture quotations in this publication are taken from the *New American Standard Bible* (NASB). © The Lockman Foundation 1960, 1962, 1963, 1968, 1971, 1972, 1973, 1975, 1977, 1995.

Printed in the United States of America

1 2 3 4 5 6 7 8 9 10 / 22 21 20 19 18 17

contents

Foreword 5

Introduction
  Why Study the Temperaments? 7

Worksheets
  Discovering Your Temperament 9

Week 1
  Thank God for the Way You Are Made 15

Week 2
  Realize Others Are Different and That's Okay 27

Week 3
  Understand How You Will Sin or Go Your Own Way 45

Week 4
  Seek to Go God's Way 61

Week 5
  Turn from Your Way by Being Filled with the Holy Spirit 77

Week 6
  Changed! A New Creation 87

Acknowledgments 100

foreword

Have you ever gotten frustrated with yourself and thought, "I wish I was more like . . .?"

Have you ever gotten frustrated with those you love and thought, "I wish they were more like . . . me?"

Have you wondered where your children came from? They are so different from you and your spouse!

Why can we say the same exact statement to two friends and get two totally different reactions?

And, honestly, do you sometimes believe others are just trying to be difficult in the way they communicate? (Whether bossy or loud or not speaking at all?!)

Trust me—this study is for you! Eleanor Lewis (who wrote this study) loved the Lord and His Word and people. Over the years, she discovered how the four temperaments impact every facet of our lives—how we process our thoughts, how we communicate with others, how we respond to situations. We are not the same! For instance, you may love to greet folks with a hug while your friends would rather shake your hand. They aren't being unfriendly—they are just different!

Simply put, people and relationships can be very puzzling at times. Consider puzzles: they come with a thousand different pieces, in various forms and colors, and they take time to piece together. They can be utterly frustrating to complete—especially when we try to force a piece into a spot where the puzzle designer never intended it to fit. The process takes patience and perseverance.

Relationships take patience, persistence, and, most importantly, love. God has told us that He, as our Creator, has fashioned each of us to be an irreplaceable piece of this amazing puzzle called "life."

> *"I will give thanks to You, for I am fearfully and wonderfully made;*
> *Wonderful are Your works,*
> *And my soul knows it very well."*
> Psalms 139:14

We were created to be unique and distinctively different. We are not the same. We are not cloned. And the Lord wants to use us for His glory in those very differences!

This is a practical study, applying God's Word to your "real" life. It will help equip you to relate to those with whom you live and work and play. If you honestly seek God and His will in this study, prepare to be amazed at how He will radically change your perception of, and perspective toward, the people He brings across your path. You will discover how to accept yourself, understand others, and like (even love) them anyway!

Enjoy sorting out the puzzle pieces of the four amazing temperaments!

Fay M. Runnion
Big Dream Ministries

introduction

Why Study the Temperaments?

Have you ever wondered why people are so different? Why don't they think correctly . . . like you? The Four Temperaments theory of behavior says we are each born with a distinct personality type that determines:

- if we are better with people or projects.
- if we want the job merely done or done right.
- if we want to enjoy life or conquer it.
- if we prefer being a spectator or a player in the game.

While we admire the strengths of each temperament, the weaknesses will cause stress in all relationships. Therefore, the purpose of this study is to enable us to:

- appreciate ourselves by recognizing our personal strengths.
- understand and accept our differences from others.
- find Biblical answers for our weaknesses and conflicts.

If you have never studied the Bible, you will be amazed at how helpful and applicable it can be. It is a fascinating book written by God through approximately forty-five people, in three languages (Hebrew, Greek, and Aramaic), on three continents (Asia, Africa, and Europe), over a period of almost 1,500 years—with one message of hope! Be sure to look up all the Bible verses cited and write down your insights.

What Is the Plan?

We will study men and women in the Bible who represent each temperament type to help us understand why we act the way we do. Because good horizontal relationships with others depend on a good vertical relationship with God, we will also seek to know what God is like and how we can have a relationship with Him.

Each lesson is divided into five study days. By devoting approximately thirty minutes a day, five days a week for six weeks, you will discover real answers for your life today.

discovering your temperament worksheets

How to Begin

1. DISCOVERING YOUR TEMPERAMENT WORKSHEET

The Temperament theory of behavior says there are four basic temperament types. We will usually find ourselves as a blend of two of these four types. To help you discover your temperament blend, you will find on page 10 a test you cannot fail!

Go down all four columns and check each word that describes you ninety-five percent of the time. Be honest! If you have trouble knowing if it's you, think back to when you were a child. You are looking for the **real** you—not what you can be but what you naturally are . . . your comfort zone.

2. UNDERSTANDING THE TEMPERAMENTS CHART

On pages 11–12, you will find charts describing the characteristics of each of the four basic temperament types.

To better understand our differences: contrast the motto and fears of each.
To better understand others: study each personality's strengths and weaknesses—overall, in relationships, and in work activities.
To better understand yourself: complete the "Discovering Your Temperament Worksheet." Then find the columns with your two larger numbers and note the letter A, B, C, or D in those two columns. Turn to pages 11–12 and carefully study the characteristics of these two personalities.

3. Now What?

You are now ready to begin the six lessons to discover insights for new beginnings in your life and relationships. Have fun!

Discovering Your Temperament Worksheet

1. Check every word in each column that describes you most of the time.
2. Count the checks in each column and put a total at the bottom.

A	B	C	D
__ Animated	__ Independent	__ Adaptable	__ Analytical
__ Easily hurt	__ Strong-willed	__ Peace-loving	__ Sensitive
__ Fun-loving	__ Outspoken	__ Quiet but fun	__ Loves detail
__ Inspiring	__ Goal-oriented	__ Easy-going	__ Thinker
__ Friendly	__ Decisive	__ Patient	__ Indecisive
__ Emotional	__ Leader	__ Listener	__ Planner
__ Talkative	__ Outgoing	__ Dependable	__ Faithful/loyal
__ Outgoing	__ Determined	__ Cool & calm	__ Precise/exact
__ Restless	__ Active	__ Teases	__ Fearful/worrier
__ Forgetful	__ Not sensitive	__ Not aggressive	__ Gifted/talented
__ Interrupts	__ Bossy/opinionated	__ Sometimes lazy	__ Perfectionist
__ Scatterbrained	__ Impatient	__ Unenthusiastic	__ Hard to please
__ Easily bored	__ Not affectionate	__ Fearful/worrier	__ Easily hurt
__ Disorganized	__ Argues/debates	__ Stubborn	__ Quiet
__ Messy	__ Gets even	__ Slow/unhurried	__ Moody
__ Quick tempered	__ Time conscious	__ Procrastinates	__ Pessimistic
Total A	**Total B**	**Total C**	**Total D**
_____	_____	_____	_____

Understanding the Temperament Chart

1. Find the columns above with your two larger scores and note the letter A, B, C, or D in those two columns.
2. Find the corresponding Personalities on pages 11–12. Carefully review these two descriptions to understand your temperament blend.

PERSONALITY A		PERSONALITY B	
Sanguine: Talker **Motto:** Let's Have Fun! **Fears:** Losing Approval		**Choleric:** Does **Motto:** I Can Do It Myself! **Fears:** Losing Control	
STRENGTHS	**WEAKNESSES**	**STRENGTHS**	**WEAKNESSES**
Overview		**Overview**	
Warm, Outgoing	Unpredictable	Confident	Anger, Revenge
Talkative	Restless	Strong-willed	Opinionated
Carefree	Spontaneous anger	Optimistic	Insensitive
Emotional	Undisciplined	Self-sufficient	Unemotional
Optimistic	Weak-willed	Not easily discouraged	Impatient
In Personal Relationships		**In Personal Relationships**	
Friendly	Undependable	Born leader	Unsympathetic
Sensitive	Poor listener	Controls	Sarcastic/Cruel
Popular	Impulsive	Exhorter	Domineering
Inspiring	Brash	Decisive	Inconsiderate
Encourager	Loud	Stimulates activity	Unforgiving
In Work Activities		**In Work Activities**	
Enthusiastic	Disorganized	Organizer	Manipulative
Natural salesman	Talks, should work	Practical	Bored with details
Good starter	Poor finisher	Goal-oriented	Demanding
Creative, good ideas	Easily distracted	Delegates work	Intolerant of errors

PERSONALITY C		PERSONALITY D	
Phlegmatic: Watcher **Motto:** Why Over-exert Myself?! **Fears:** Losing Peace		**Melancholy:** Thinker **Motto:** If It is Worth Doing, Do It Right! **Fears:** Making a Mistake	
STRENGTHS	**WEAKNESSES**	**STRENGTHS**	**WEAKNESSES**
Overview		**Overview**	
Calm, Relaxed	Unenthusiastic	Gifted, Genius prone	Moody/Depressive
Easy-going	Worrier/fearful	Analytical	Pessimistic/Negative
Patient, Kind	Pessimistic	Sensitive	Too introspective
Peace-loving	Compromising	Deep and thoughtful	Hypochondria
In Personal Relationships		**In Personal Relationships**	
Likable	Stingy	Self-disciplined	Critical, Picky
Dry, witty humor	Selfish	Dependable, Loyal	Unsociable
Good listener	Stubborn	Self-sacrificing	Remembers past
Faithful friend	Indifferent	Faithful friend	Sulks
In Work Activities		**In Work Activities**	
Good under pressure	Procrastinates	Perfectionist, Intellectual	Theoretical
Adaptable	Unmotivated	Conscientious	Tires easily
Practical, Finds easy way	Indecisive	Likes detail work	Hard to please
Steady, Reliable	Reluctant leader	Finds creative solution	Indecisive
Efficient planner	Spectator	Likes charts, graphs	Plans too much

key to symbols

Talker
Sanguine: SUN—Sanguines have a sunny disposition

Doer
Choleric: CROWN—Cholerics like to be king of the hill

Watcher
Phlegmatic: DOVE—Phlegmatics desire peace at all times

Thinker
Melancholy: HEART—Biblically, the heart and mind are synonymous and Melancholies are thinkers

Bible verse to memorize:
MEMORIZE

Important thought:
IMPORTANT THOUGHT **Insight, found at the end of each day:** When an insight is applied to your life, you will be changed from a caterpillar to a butterfly.

Quick Study:
- **QS** QuickStudy: Shortened study for busy days.

Week ONE

thank God for the way you are made

SANGUINE

AN OUTGOING PEOPLE PERSON— THE TALKER

Have you ever wished you were somebody else? Given the opportunity, most of us would change ourselves in some way. Not tall enough? Envious of your friend's organizational abilities? It is natural to focus on what we look like, what we have, and what we don't have. It is also natural to compare ourselves with others, but it usually makes us feel inferior because we tend to focus on others' strengths and our own weaknesses.

Because it is not natural to accept ourselves, how can we *see our value*?

DAY 1—Meet the Sanguine

To better understand and appreciate ourselves and others, the first four weeks of this course will focus on the four temperament types. Weeks five and six will give answers for overcoming our weaknesses. Let's start by looking at two Sanguines. Remember, Sanguines are delightful, sunny people who enjoy life. Their motto is "Let's have fun."

1. Meet Sanguine Rebekah
   God chose Abraham to be the father of a great nation through whom He would send the Savior of the world. Abraham, a man of great wealth and position, sent his servant to another country to find a wife for his son Isaac. The servant met a beautiful young woman named Rebekah at a well.

SANGUINE

AN OUTGOING PEOPLE PERSON— THE TALKER

Greatest strengths: Friendly, Charming, Influences people, Enthusiastic, Compassionate, Positive thinker. Sees the bright side. Creative, Emotional. Talks easily with strangers. Spontaneous. Decisions are usually based on feelings or emotions.

Greatest weaknesses: Disorganized. May not finish tasks. Big ego. Needs constant approval. Doesn't learn from the past. Spontaneously responds to all external stimuli. Acts without plan or forethought. Inconsistent. Undisciplined. Stretches the truth. Weak-willed.

Strengths overdone become weaknesses: Their spontaneity uncontrolled becomes the weakness of disorder.

15

- **Genesis 24:15–28, 55–58** In spite of the different culture and treatment of women, record examples of Rebekah's Sanguine qualities.

As a Sanguine, Rebekah talked easily with a stranger. Because Sanguines desire to please, she sought approval by giving this man a drink and inviting him home for the night. Sanguines enjoy a spontaneous party! Only a Sanguine who talks and acts without forethought would agree to leave home, go to a foreign land, and marry a complete stranger—immediately!

2. Rebekah married Abraham's son Isaac and had twin sons, Jacob and Esau. Esau was an adventuresome, dramatic, spontaneous Sanguine much like his mother, while Jacob was a quiet, laid-back Phlegmatic very much her opposite.

   - **Genesis 25:27–28** Which son did Rebekah prefer, the one like or unlike herself?

3. Often we have trouble with people who are too much like us because we see our own weaknesses in them. Rather, we may be attracted to those who are unlike us, because we see and admire their strengths—which we don't have. Rebekah was attracted to Phlegmatic Jacob because he was a mild-mannered, quiet man. As a talker, she probably enjoyed this listener, and she may have felt he needed her to motivate and inspire him.

   - **Genesis 25:29–34** What did Esau's Sanguine, live-for-the-moment, nature cost him?

4. Because Sanguines are controlled by present circumstances, they often fail to think of future consequences. When hungry, Esau sold his inheritance for a bowl of soup!
   Sanguines are born persuaders who can sell their ideas or the proverbial ice to Eskimos. However, they have one problem. They may exaggerate or even lie to make the sale.

   - **Genesis 27:41–45** What is the reason Rebekah wanted Jacob to go away?

- **Genesis 27:46** What reason does she give her husband Isaac?

Instead of communicating truth, Sanguines (and sometimes the rest of us) may stretch the truth or manipulate to get what they (we) want. The sad result for Rebekah was that the few days Jacob was to stay away became twenty years. She never saw her dear son again!

 Each Temperament has strengths and weaknesses. We need to appreciate our strengths and realize that our weaknesses will create painful problems in all of our relationships.

DAY 2—Meet Sanguine Peter

1. In Rebekah, we saw the friendly, spontaneous nature of the Sanguine. Tim LaHaye points out in his book *Transformed Temperaments* that Peter is the most wonderful example of a charismatic Sanguine extrovert in the Bible. Peter shows that being spontaneous or impetuous can be both good and bad.

   - **QS Matthew 4:18–20** What did Peter do impetuously?

2. It was good for Peter to follow Jesus as Jesus invites each of us to follow Him. However, Sanguines not only act impulsively, they often talk impulsively as well. Unfortunately, they may act and speak *before* they think.

   - **QS Matthew 17:1–4** Did anyone ask Peter a question?

   - **QS Matthew 17:4** What did Peter do anyway?

- **QS Matthew 17:5** What does God say Peter should do instead of talk?

3. When Simon Peter listened to Jesus he came to two conclusions:
   - **QS Luke 5:8, 11** What did Peter conclude about himself?

   - **QS Matthew 16:13–17** What did Peter conclude about Jesus?

   - **QS Matthew 1:21** Why did Jesus come to earth?

   - **QS Matthew 16:21–22** In spite of Peter's understanding that Jesus is the Christ, the Messiah or Savior, what does Peter do?

As much as Sanguines like to talk, they don't like discussing unpleasant things. Therefore, when Jesus spoke of his need to suffer and die to save us from our sins, Peter told Jesus He was making a mistake.

- Have you ever told God He is making a mistake? When?

4. Sanguines are delightful and always have something to say, but sometimes they need to listen and not feel obligated to fill all silences. When Peter listened, he realized that even though he was a follower of Jesus, he was still a sinner. He also realized that Jesus is the Christ, the Savior of sinners.

- **QS** **1 John 1:8–10** What did Peter need to do?

- **QS** **1 John 1:9** If we confess or agree with God about our sin, what does God promise?

- Have you ever confessed you were a sinner and asked Jesus to forgive and cleanse you? When?

Insight Day 2

We call them weaknesses, but God calls them sins. Doesn't weakness sound better?

Jesus died to pay for our sins. Our part is to confess or agree that we have sinned. God's part is to forgive and cleanse us. When He has done so much for us, why do we accuse Him of making mistakes?

DAY 3—Meet Yourself

1. Am I an accident or a mistake?
   My son Travis was born with a severe birth defect—his stomach and intestinal tract were outside his body. Was this an accident or a mistake? Are you?

   - **Exodus 4:10–12** Are your imperfections accidents? What did God make?

   - **Psalms 100:3** Who made you?

- **Psalms 139:13–14** How were you made? What does it mean when the Scripture says you are "fearfully and wonderfully" made? The Old Testament was written in Hebrew, and the word translated "fearfully" means awesome, and "wonderfully" means distinct or distinguished to make a difference.

- What then is God saying about you?

IMPORTANT THOUGHT As much as the world tempts you to be dissatisfied with who you are or how you look, you are not an accident or a mistake. God designed you to be awesomely, distinctively unique in your appearance and your personality. He distinguished you to make a difference.

2. Okay, I'm not a mistake but does God know about me?

   - **QS** **Psalms 139:13, 16** Where were you when God first knew you?

   - **QS** **Psalms 139:1–4** What does God know about you? Make a list.

   - **QS** **Psalms 139:17–18** Does God ever think about you? How many thoughts?

   - **Jeremiah 29:11** What kind of thoughts does He think?

3. Does God care about me?

- **Jeremiah 31:3** Why is God interested in you?

- **Jeremiah 1:4–5** When did God's plan for Jeremiah begin?

- **Jeremiah 1:5–8** Was God's plan specific? What was Jeremiah to do?

- What is God saying about His plan for you?

God's plan for Jeremiah: to be a prophet to the nations.
God's plan for Rebekah: to raise sons who would be the line of Jesus.
God's plan for Peter: to hear and speak only God's words of truth.
God's plan for You: _____.

You are always in God's thoughts and His plans. God's plan for each of us is different, but He does have a specific plan for your life—one to give you a future and a hope.

DAY 4—My Response

1. How should I respond?
   We are not unknown faces or numbers to God. He specially formed us in our mother's wombs. Therefore, our parents, appearance, abilities, lack of abilities or disabilities, are not mistakes. Before we were in the womb, God already had a plan for us. In the womb, He formed us with everything we need to accomplish that plan.

- **Psalms 139:14** How did David respond to God for the way he was made?

- How should you respond for the way you are made?

- **Romans 9:20–21** Instead of giving thanks for the way we are, what is our usual response?

2. Words or deeds?
    When Travis was born, I thought God was punishing me for my sin. I picked up the Bible for the first time, and God assured me through John 9:3 that He was not punishing me. Instead, He would show me His power. I had to trust God's Word and praise Him for the way Travis was made.

    - **QS** **John 14:15, 21** What proves we love God?

    We may tell God with words that we trust Him, thank Him, or love Him, but God says real love is demonstrated by obedience to Him. In other words, it is not what we **say** but what we **do**. Words can be easier than actions for all of us but especially for Sanguines. They often have good intentions, but may lack the discipline or self-control to follow through with their good intentions.

    - **Matthew 26:31–35** How did Peter "say" he would respond to Jesus?

    - **Matthew 26:69–75** How did Peter respond instead?

3. Fruit is the Answer
   Like Peter, we often have good intentions but lack the power to do what we should.

   - **QS Galatians 5:22–25** What are the qualities God wants in our life? Make a list.

   - What does God call all these qualities?

   - Who will produce this "fruit" in your life? How?

   - **Ephesians 1:12–13** How do I get the Holy Spirit?

4. Fruit Inspecting
   Most of us think a Christian is a religious person who follows rules—do's and don'ts. However, God's definition of a Christian is someone who has Christ's Spirit in them making them fruitful people not "religious nuts." God's Spirit will produce in us God's character qualities or fruit of: *love, joy, peace, patience, goodness, kindness, faithfulness, humility,* and *self-control*.

   SANGUINES need self-control   **CHOLERICS need love**
   PHLEGMATICS need peace   **MELANCHOLIES need joy**

   - Which of these nine character qualities or fruit did Rebekah and Peter lack?

- Which of these nine qualities do you often lack?

5. Cultivating Fruit

Though we can thank God for the way we are made, it is obvious there are some things about us that need to be changed. We aren't always loving, kind, self-controlled, joyful, or obedient—but we want to be!

> **IMPORTANT THOUGHT** This fruit cannot be manufactured by self-effort but can only be grown in us by God when conditions are right in our lives.

- **QS** **John 15:1–5** What must you do to be fruitful?

- **2 Corinthians 5:17** What will happen if you receive Christ and abide in Him?

When we receive Jesus, God plants the seed of His Word and His Spirit in us. As we abide in Jesus, He cultivates fruit in our life. We are like soil. God's Word is the seed, and our trials and choices are the tools—the hoe and shovel—God uses to till the soil so that we bear fruit.

Tools God might use in the life of a:

SANGUINE

A temptation—to produce His fruit of self-control

CHOLERIC

Slow people or delays—to produce His fruit of patience

PHLEGMATIC

Conflict—to produce His fruit of peace

MELANCHOLY

Imperfect people or situations—to produce the fruit of joy

• What difficulty are you facing right now that God can use to improve you?

Insight Day 4

God made me wonderfully, but He wants to remake those qualities about me that aren't so wonderful.

When I receive Jesus, He forgives me and seals me with His Holy Spirit, Who will change me from the inside out.

DAY 5—New Insights Lead to New Beginnings

1. New Insights
   a. What did you learn about Sanguines this week?

   b. What encouraged you most as you looked at yourself from God's point of view?

   c. What did God's Word reveal about you and your value?

   d. What new insights did you receive about God this week?

   e. What does Psalms 139:14 mean to you now?

2. New Beginnings Start with God's Word
   MEMORIZE Psalms 139:14a:

   "I will give thanks to you, for I am fearfully and wonderfully made."

3. New Beginnings Take Action
   Write down three things you like about yourself: that you are a good communicator, leader, thinker, or diplomat; that you are good with computers, people, numbers, machines, ideas, music, color, or your hands; you are practical, creative, loyal, or fun.

   1.

   2.

   3.

Spend a few moments thanking God for these three qualities. Resist those negative thoughts because we are thanking God for what we can do, not what we can't—what we are, not what we aren't. Stop comparing yourself to others. Remember you are distinguished to make a difference.

Insight Day 5

We need to thank God for making us special with both strengths and weaknesses. Weaknesses have value, because they show us our need for a Savior.

Religious effort is not enough. Like Peter, I must acknowledge, "I am a sinner, and Jesus is the Savior." I must invite Him into my life to forgive me and change me from the inside out.

Would you like to admit your need and receive Jesus' forgiveness? Why not turn the Day 5 Insight into your personal prayer to God right now?

Week TWO

realize others are different and that's okay

Greatest strengths:
Born leader,
Goal-oriented,
Productive,
Determined,
Takes a stand,
Organizer, Decisive,
Active, Persistent,
Independent,
Practical,
Confident, Bottom-
liner, Competitive,
Strong-willed,
Makes decisions by
act of the will

Greatest weaknesses:
Opinionated,
Insensitive,
Impatient,
Sarcastic, Blunt,
Self-willed, Angry,
Demanding,
Wounds those
they are gifted to
lead, Workaholic,
Goals may come
before people,
Unemotional,
Emotionally
challenged,
Self-sufficient

Strengths overdone become weaknesses: Their leadership and strong opinions uncontrolled become bossiness and dictatorship.

Remember the old saying "opposites attract?" As a Choleric-Sanguine, I was always attracted to Phlegmatic-Melancholies because they have strengths where I have weaknesses. I fell in love with wonderful Phlegmatic-Melancholy, Bob, because he was so agreeable and easy-going. After marriage, however, I discovered that, each night after work, he would lay on the sofa "to recharge his batteries." As a Choleric-Sanguine, I was born with charged batteries! Although we need each other, we have built-in conflict. He needs me to light his fire; I need him to put mine out. (Cholerics tend to be workaholics.)

Opposites do attract but very often the very characteristic that attracts you early in a relationship is the one that most annoys you later. For example, the:

- **SANGUINE's delightfully spontaneity** . . . later seems to be annoying disorder
- **CHOLERIC's admirable decisiveness** . . . quickly feels like controlling bossiness
- **PHLEGMATIC's calming, unrushed nature** . . . can become irritating inertia
- **MELANCHOLY's wonderful sensitivity** . . . soon becomes deflating pickiness

Last week we saw that our natural tendency is to complain about the way we are made. It should not be surprising that we also have a difficult time accepting the way others are made, especially those close to us. We pray for God to change them—or we set out to do it ourselves. We believe if they would think correctly (like me), life would be better!

> To live above with Saints we love,
> That will be glory.
> But to live here below with Saints we know,
> Well, that's a different story!!
> (old Irish saying)

Why can't we get along?

DAY 1—Meet the Choleric

According to last week's Insight, we can thank God for the way we are made. We can appreciate ourselves because God made us unique and has a special plan for each of us. This week we will think about why we have so much difficulty in relationships. We will start by looking at the Choleric who has an especially difficult time with relationships because the Choleric motto is "I can do it myself!"

1. Meet Choleric Martha
    Jesus owned no property and had "no place to lay his head," so He spent time in the home of his good friend Martha, and her sister Mary, and their brother Lazarus.

    * **Luke 10:38–42** List examples of Martha's good and bad Choleric qualities.

Martha is a doer. You never find her sitting around. She is always getting things done. Cholerics are project-oriented. However, Martha's project—preparing a meal for friends—became more important than the friends themselves. She grumbled or became angry when others didn't work as hard or do as much as she did. We all might have had the same thought as Martha, "Lord, don't you care?"—but only a strong-willed Choleric would be bold enough to verbalize it.

Last week, we saw that Sanguine Peter followed Jesus but did not trust Him. He told Jesus what to do.

Choleric Martha believed in Jesus, but she didn't trust Him either. *Trust is critical to any relationship!*

Later, Martha personally experienced Jesus' power when He raised her brother Lazarus from the dead (John 11). Of course, in true choleric fashion, she verbally challenged Jesus. "If you had been here, my brother wouldn't have died. Yes, Jesus, I believe You can raise him from the dead, but we can't roll away the stone as you command because by now he stinks!" Cholerics always have to get in the last word—even with God—and even when they are wrong.

- **John 12:1–3** As Martha learned to trust Jesus, He changed her. What is Martha doing? Is she complaining?

God changed this Choleric by producing the fruit of patience and gentleness in her. This family is a picture of what God desires for us: Martha served Jesus without complaint. Lazarus sat with Him in fellowship. Mary anointed His feet in worship.

- In doing this Bible study, you are spending time in fellowship with God so that you can serve and worship Him. Are you grumbling?

2. Meet Choleric Paul
   Before Saul (later known as Paul) trusted Jesus, he was a very religious person who was always *doing* something. Like many of us, his beliefs were sincere, but he was sincerely wrong.

   - **Acts 7:58–8:3; 26:4–5, 9–11** Describe Saul/Paul's actions before he encountered Jesus.

His actions reflected his wrong thinking. He was cruel, he persecuted Christians, and he participated in murder. Remember God says, "If you love Me, you'll obey Me." Even when doing wrong, Cholerics do it with gusto!

- **QS Acts 26:12–15** How did Paul meet Jesus?

- **QS** **Acts 26:16–20** What was God's plan for Paul? Make a list.

- **QS** **Acts 26:18, 20** What "turning" is necessary to have your sins forgiven?

Repent means to change directions—to be so sorry for going my own way that I am willing to turn (change directions) and go God's way. It is to turn from self to God.

3. Lead, follow, or get out of the way!
Both Sanguines and Cholerics talk and lead, but their methods are very different. Sanguines lead by inspiring; Cholerics lead by commanding.

Our temperament weaknesses are never an excuse to sin!

Being SANGUINE—is not an excuse for disorder.
Being CHOLERIC—is not an excuse for bluntness.
Being PHLEGMATIC—is not an excuse for laziness.
Being MELANCHOLY—is not an excuse for moodiness.

- **Acts 27:1–2** In what situation is Paul?

- **Acts 27:9–36** Paul is a prisoner but who is leading: Paul or the guard?

Cholerics are natural-born leaders who take over every situation. They have to be in control. They have a compulsion to tell you what they think even when you don't want to know. They convince or intimidate you to do it their way—now! Unfortunately, their way may not be best because, in their haste to act, they often neglect details. Cholerics push people but when pushed:

SANGUINES get angry.
CHOLERICS push back.
PHLEGMATICS get stubborn.
MELANCHOLIES get hurt.

the amazing temperaments

Choleric weaknesses leave a path of destruction in all their relationships. Even Choleric children are a challenge. Parents of Cholerics must resist over-controlling the child as Cholerics need to be in charge of something. However, parents must not be controlled by the child or they may lose their authority and the child's respect.

- **Ephesians 6:1–3** What are parents to teach their children to do and why?

Insight Day 1

We need to realize others are different. It's not a matter of right and wrong, we're just different.
Don't expect others to think as you think or feel as you feel.
Remember, God made them fearfully and wonderfully, too! Therefore, realize others are different and know that's okay. Revise your expectations!

DAY 2—The Godhead is Different!

1. Different Views and Different Ways
   Each temperament can look at the same thing and see it differently.

Views on Going Fishing:

> **SANGUINE's goal:** to enjoy—telling fish stories
> **CHOLERIC's goal:** to catch a fish—standing at the front of the boat
> **PHLEGMATIC's goal:** to relax—laying in the back of the boat
> **MELANCHOLY's goal:** to do it right—studying a manual on "how to fish"

Our differences do not keep us from doing anything. It just means the way we do it will differ from the way another temperament would. For example, we have had Presidents of the United States of all four temperament types.

Ways of Presiding:

SANGUINE Ronald Reagan: a leader through inspiration. He told wonderful, motivated stories. He didn't always get his facts straight, but he made us feel good! He wasn't on top of details but he made meetings enjoyable, eating jelly beans! (Nancy was probably a Melancholy.)

CHOLERIC Richard Nixon: a leader through intimidation. He became president through Choleric persistence. Though soundly defeated previously, he didn't quit. He had opinions and didn't care who agreed. He was decisive and unemotional even when he was kicked out of office. He had only one close friend (Cholerics don't need many) and a faithful Phlegmatic wife.

PHLEGMATIC Gerald Ford: a leader by default but just the man for the job at the time. After Nixon's demise, the country needed a steady, reliable peacemaker to rebuild trust. Ford didn't offend or rock the boat. Like Eisenhower, another Phlegmatic, Ford played lots of golf. His wife (probably Choleric-Melancholy) in some ways made a bigger impact than he did as she did something about her addiction problem and then helped others.

MELANCHOLY Jimmy Carter: a leader by thinking. He kept impeccable notes—his library is twice the size of Reagan's, though he was in office half the length of time. He labored over decisions. When the hostages were taken in Iran, he appeared indecisive because he feared making a mistake. A Choleric would have done something—probably bombed them! However, if Melancholy Carter had been President instead of Sanguine Reagan, we never would have had Irangate because he would have been on top of all the details. Carter's Choleric wife was criticized for taking part in his administration, but a Choleric has to be involved.

2. God's Answer
   Even with understanding, we still may have trouble getting along. Is there an answer?

   * **Mark 12:30–31** Who are we to love and in what order?

IMPORTANT THOUGHT I am to love you as I love me—but I can't love you until I love me. I can't love me until I love the Lord—but I can't love the Lord until I know what He is like.

3. What is God like?
   Just as each of us was created differently, there is diversity in the Godhead. God is one God in three Persons, which is a very difficult concept to understand. Someone has said, "Try to understand the Trinity and you'll lose your mind but disregard the Trinity and you'll lose your soul." Each person of the Godhead relates to us in a unique and personal way so that we might see how to relate to God and others in appropriate ways.

   * **QS** **2 Corinthians 13:14** What is the role of:

   1. God the Son—Jesus

2. God the Father

3. God the Holy Spirit

- **Philippians 2:1** What does Christ's grace bring?

What does God's love bring?

What does the Spirit's fellowship bring?

- **Philippians 2:1–4** As you experience Christ's consolation, God's comfort, and the Spirit's compassion, how are you then free to act toward others? Make a list.

The key to good horizontal relationships with others is a good vertical relationship with the entire Godhead! We need to know God.

4. Meet God the Father
   We resist the love of the Father because we don't understand what He is like.

   - **1 John 4:7–8** Does God love? Why?

   - **Romans 5:8–10** How do we know God is love?

   - **Romans 8:35–39** When we accept God's love, what can separate us from it?

   - **Romans 11:33–36** Is God wise? What does He know?

   - **I Chronicles 29: 11–14** Is God sovereign? What does He control?

5. God the Father is loving, wise, and sovereign. What is true about Jesus?

   - **Ephesians 3:19, 5:2** Does Jesus love? How do you know?

   - **I Corinthians 1:24** Is Jesus wise?

- **I Timothy 6:14–15** Is Jesus sovereign?

Jesus has the exact same qualities as the Father because Jesus is God. When we look at Jesus, we see what God is like. Many view God only as Love. Others see Him only as a vindictive Judge waiting to punish. The truth is that God is both loving and just. In His holiness, He must judge sin but, in His love, He loves the sinner. Therefore, in love, God sent Jesus to pay the judgment for our sin thus satisfying His own holiness.

Insight Day 2

Why do I fear trusting God? Why do I question His ways when God is:
- LOVE and wants what is best!
- WISE and knows what is best!
- SOVEREIGN and does what is best.

DAY 3—Meet Jesus

1. Who is Jesus?

I have often wondered why the name *Jesus* is such a common curse word. Why don't people say, "Oh, Buddha!" or "Oh, Mohammed!" Why is Jesus' name so different? New parents carefully pick the perfect name for their child because names are the labels we carry through life. In Biblical times, names were even more important, because they were not just a label but a description of the character of the person.

- **QS** **Matthew 1:20–21** Mary is having a baby. What is His name? What does it mean?

- **QS** **Matthew 1:22–23** Jesus had another name. What is it? What does it mean?

- **QS** **Acts 4:10, 12** What is true about the name of Jesus?

God is so great that one name can't adequately describe His character, so He has many names:

> **Jehovah Rapha:** the God who heals
> **Jehovah Jireh:** the God who provides
> **Jehovah Shalom:** the God our peace-giver
> **El Shaddai:** the Almighty God or all-sufficient One who is all I need
> **El Elyon:** the Most High God who controls all things
> **The Lord, The Savior, The Shepherd, Immanuel, Jesus, etc. . . .**

2. Is Jesus really "Immanuel, God with Us?"
   What did Jesus claim about Himself? Record His claims below:

   • **QS** John 5:17–18

   • **QS** John 10:30–33

   • **QS** John 14:6

   • **QS** John 14:9

3. Did Jesus prove He is God?
   Many have claimed to be God, though neither Buddha nor Mohammed did. It is one thing to claim to be God but quite another to prove it. Record your insights on the following chart.

   What did Jesus do? How did people respond?

	WHAT DID JESUS DO?	HOW DID PEOPLE RESPOND?
John 4:29, 39–42		
John 5:5–9, 15–16		
John 6:5–14		
John 11:43–46, 53		
John 20:26–28		

People had two very different responses to the miracles of Jesus. Some called Him Lord and surrendered to Him. Others persecuted and plotted against Him. Today some think, "If I could see Jesus or a miracle, I would believe." Yet these people saw, and some walked away unbelieving. Jesus did what only God can do—heal the sick and raise the dead. He gives us a choice. Will you believe He is God, or will you walk away?

4. What does the Bible claim about Jesus?

  • QS **Colossians 1:13–14; 2:10, 13–14** What did or will Jesus do for you?

- **QS Colossians 1:15–17** What did Jesus do for the world?

- **QS Colossians 2:8–9** Who is Jesus?

- **Titus 2:13** What will Jesus do in the future?

5. What are other names of Jesus?

   - **Isaiah 9:6** Make a list.

   - If names describe character, what do these names say about Jesus?

   - What do they say about the place Jesus should have in your life?

Jesus is God with us.

He is equal with God the Father.

His names reveal the relationship He desires to have with you. He wants to be your:

- *Savior* from eternal hopelessness.
- *Lord* in a confusing world.
- *Counselor* who knows all things.
- *Mighty God* when you are powerless.
- *Eternal Father* when you feel alone.
- *Prince of Peace* in the midst of chaos.

DAY 4—Why Do I Need Jesus?

1. What frees us in relationships?

Over the door of many libraries are the words, "You shall know the truth, and the truth shall set you free." The implication is that, if I read the books, I will be free, that knowledge brings freedom. However, I may be highly educated and not be free at all. *What does free us?*

- **2 Timothy 3:1–5** What did God warn would happen in the last days?

- **2 Timothy 3:7** What does God warn that people will be doing?

- **1 Corinthians 8:1b** What can knowledge do?

- **QS John 17:17** What is truth?

- **QS John 8:31–32a** What must I do to know truth?

- **QS** John 8:32b What does truth do?

- **QS** John 8:34–36 What does Jesus do?

- **QS** John 14:6 What can Jesus free you from? Who is truth?

- **QS** Romans 6:22; 8:2 From what does Jesus free you?

It is truth, not knowledge, that frees us! God's Word is the written truth pointing us to Jesus, the living Truth.

2. How must I respond?
    Jesus offers Himself as the Truth that sets you free from sin and condemnation.
        What must I do in response to this knowledge? Record insights below.

- **Matthew 18:2–3**

- **QS** John 1:12–13

- **John 3:3, 5–6**

- **QS** **Acts 2:21**

- **QS** **Acts 16:30–31** (*Believe* means: adhere to, trust in, and rely on*)*

- **Revelation 3:20**

Insight Day 4

Freedom comes from knowing truth.
We must believe Jesus is God, the Truth, and invite Him to control our lives. He stands at the door of our heart and knocks, but because the only doorknob is on the inside of the door, we must open the door and invite Him in. No decision is a decision!

DAY 5—God's Insights Lead to New Beginnings

1. New Insights
   a. What new insights did you learn about Cholerics this week?

   b. What did you learn about Jesus?

   c. What did you learn about yourself?

d. How does knowing the names or character of Jesus affect your attitude toward Him?

- **Philippians 2:9–11** What does God say about Jesus' name?

e. What one truth is God asking you to apply this week?

2. New Beginnings Start with God's Word
   MEMORIZE Mark 12:29b-31

> *"The Lord our God is one Lord; and You shall love the Lord Your God with all your heart, and with all your soul, and with all your mind, and with all your strength . . . You shall love your neighbor as yourself."*

3. New Beginnings Take Action
   a. Realize others are different and that's okay.

   b. Revise your expectations. Don't expect others to think like you think. Don't expect them not to disappoint you. We all sin, we all disappoint, and we all will fail.

   c. Let Jesus change your responses to meet the special needs of others.

   SANGUINES need: praise, attention, freedom to be spontaneous.
   CHOLERICS need: control, activity, for you to get to the point.
   PHLEGMATICS need: comfort, recognition of their quiet efforts, routines.
   MELANCHOLIES need: information, time to analyze it, encouragement.

   d. Learn to laugh together about your differences! Don't take yourself too seriously. Enjoy those people God has brought into your life.

the amazing temperaments

e. Write down the names of two people close to you with whom you have conflict. What is one quality they have that you need to accept, appreciate, and encourage? Tell them today how much you value them.

Name	Quality to appreciate
1. _____	_____
2. _____	_____

Insight Day 5

Right now, thank God for all those with whom you are in relationship.
    Thank Him that you are better together than you are separately because your strengths cover each others' weaknesses.
    Ask God to keep you focused on others' strengths and not on their weaknesses. Remember, we are different, and that's okay—so revise your expectations!

Week THREE

understand how you will sin or go your own way

Greatest strengths:
Naturally nice,
Easy to get along
with, Patient,
Steady, Laid back,
Persistent, Kind,
Thoughtful, Good
listener, Diplomatic,
Inventive,
Finds easy way,
Thinks jobs
through, Works
under pressure,
Dependable,
Efficient

I was married less than forty-eight hours when I knew I'd made a big mistake. (I'm sure Bob felt the same!) The honeymoon revealed our temperament weaknesses. There was no bridal suite because easy-going Mr. Phlegmatic hadn't planned ahead. I discovered Phlegmatics are quietly strong-willed, and there is nothing worse than a Choleric being with someone they can't control. The honeymoon was over before it got started. I felt like Ruth Graham who said, "Lord, if you forgive me for marrying him, I promise I'll never do it again!"

Last week's insight showed us that we first must have a relationship with the Lord in order to have good relationships with others. It is only through the Lord that we are free to love ourselves and others. Knowing the temperaments is a help as we appreciate and understand our differences, but there are times when we just have trouble getting along. Is our problem that we are so different, or is it that we actually are the same? We are the same in that we all want to have our own way!

**Greatest
Weaknesses:**
Unenthusiastic,
Procrastinator,
Selfish with
time/energy,
Unmotivated,
May not live up to
great potential,
Takes easy way
out, Stubborn,
Uninvolved, Resists
change, Comfort
rules, Quietly
strong-willed, Slow,
Not aggressive

**Strengths Can
Become
Weaknesses:**
Their laid back,
easy-going nature
uncontrolled
becomes laziness!

DAY 1—Meet the Phlegmatic

Life is a series of choices. Which way should we go? What choice is right? This week we will look at two Phlegmatics to see the consequences of choices they made. The Phlegmatic motto is: Why over-exert myself?

1. Meet Phlegmatic Hannah

   Hannah was married to a man named Elkanah and lived at a time of great ungodliness. It was a time when everyone did what seemed right in his own eyes. It was probably a lot like today! Hebrew women greatly desired children because they knew God had promised to send a special Son who would bring Holy God and unholy men together.

   - **1 Samuel 1:5–8** What was Hannah's problem?

   A Sanguine or Choleric with the problem of being childless would have been emotional, angry, and verbal: "It's my husband's fault; it's God's fault." They would have blamed others and would have been noisy about it.

   - **1 Samuel 1:9–13** What did Phlegmatic Hannah do instead? Was she noisy?

   Hannah prayed a very specific prayer. Faith is *hearing* God's Word, *believing* and *obeying* it, *without seeing* the end result.

   - **1 Samuel 1:15–18** Did Hannah have faith? How do you know?

   Though not yet pregnant, Hannah believed God's Word; therefore, she ate and had joy before the answer came. She believed and obeyed without seeing.

   - **1 Samuel 1:19–20; 2:20–21** How did God reward Hannah's faith?

2. Meet Phlegmatic Abraham

   Abraham lived around 2,000 BC in Ur, one of the outstanding cities of that day. It was the center of manufacturing, commerce, and trade. It had large houses with ten to twenty rooms, libraries, indoor plumbing, and a city sewer system. Education was advanced, but the city was wicked. The people worshipped the moon goddess and were into astrology and witchcraft. In spite of the ungodly society around him, Abraham developed a deep faith or trust in the one true God. Even though God spoke to him, Abraham had to learn to trust God enough to obey Him.

- **Acts 7:2–4** While Abraham was in Ur, God spoke to him. What was he to do?

- **Genesis 11:31–32, 12:4–5** Did Abraham leave his family? Did Abraham exhibit faith?

Instead of Abraham leaving his father, his father Terah took Abraham! Terah means *delay*, and they did delay in Haran until Terah died. Then God spoke again.

- **Genesis 12:2–3** What was God's plan for Abraham? Make a list.

Phlegmatics are warm, family people who enjoy security and dislike change though they adapt very well to it. God told Abraham to leave his family and land and go where God would show him. This certainly required faith. We admire Abraham for packing the bags and going.

However, clinging to his security, Abraham only partially obeyed. He did not leave his father and nephew but took them along! Then he delayed obeying. God was moving Abraham to Canaan, but Abraham stopped along the way in Haran and stayed there until his father Terah died. Remember:

Partial obedience or delayed obedience is really disobedience!

Abraham finally left Haran for Canaan but took his nephew Lot with him (Gen.12:1–4). Phlegmatics may not do all or become all they could because of fear and self-protection. They guard their time, energy, space, and comfort!

4. Consequences of Bad Choices
   Abraham and Sarah are a typical married couple . . . opposites attract! Sarah appears to be a Choleric-Melancholy blend, and Abraham is probably a Phlegmatic-Sanguine.

- **Genesis 15:5** What did God promise Abraham and Sarah?

- **Genesis 16:1–3** With whom did Phlegmatic Abraham attempt to avoid conflict?

- **Genesis 16:4** What was the resulting bad choice and its immediate effect?

- **Genesis 16:4,6** How did that choice affect other people?

- **Genesis 16:5** In typical Choleric (or is it human?) fashion, what does Sarah do?

James 4:17 says sin is what we do and what we don't do. Abraham sinned both ways.

He didn't: listen to the voice of God.
He did: listen to the voice of his impatient Choleric wife instead.
He didn't: trust God to keep His promise of giving a son.
He did: trust having an affair in order to help God out.

- **Genesis 18:10–14; 21:1–3** Did God need Abraham's help?

- Does God need your help? Can you think of a time you acted instead of trusted?

The consequence of Abraham's sin was strained relationships—the very thing he was trying to avoid. Ishmael was born of his affair with the handmaid, and Isaac was the God-given son of his wife Sarah. If Abraham had trusted God, we all would have been spared much strife because Ishmael became the forefather of the Arabs, and Isaac was a forefather of the Jews. The two have had conflicts to this very day. Consequences of choices go on and on!

Insight Day 1

All choices have consequences—good and bad. Galatians 6:7 says we reap what we sow.

"Sin will take you farther than you want to go, keep you longer than you want to stay, and cost you more than you want to pay." (Ravi Zacharias)

Be careful of those choices!

DAY 2—Meet the Real Problem

1. Though we are different, are we the same?
As we study the Temperaments, we realize we are born with very distinct and different outlooks on life.

> **SANGUINES** . . . talk and enjoy.
> **CHOLERICS** . . . do and control.
> **PHLEGMATICS** . . . watch and make peace.
> **MELANCHOLIES** . . . think and seek perfection.

But is there anything about us that is the same?

- **QS Romans 3:10–12, 23** What is the same about every person? Make a list.

2. What is sin?
When Sanguine Peter was in Jesus' presence, he saw himself as a sinner. Choleric Paul said, "Jesus came into this world to save sinners of whom I am chief." Now we see we are all sinners!

What is sin? Record insights from these scriptures:

- **Isaiah 30:1** What do we do that is sin?

- **QS Isaiah 53:6** Whose way do we go when we sin?

- **QS** Romans 14:23(b)

- **QS** James 4:17

- **QS** 1 John 3:4

- **Matthew 7:21–23** Does sin/iniquity necessarily look bad? What were the people doing that Jesus called iniquity?

- Based on these verses, write a definition of sin. Is sin limited to our actions?

3. Will all sin look alike?
   The temperament study shows us that all sin does not look the same. Sin is going our own way, and the way each of the four temperaments wants to go is different.

   SANGUINES want . . . the fun way.
   CHOLERICS want . . . my way.
   PHLEGMATICS want . . . the easy way.
   MELANCHOLIES want . . . the right way (as they define *right*).

- Why is it easier to see sin in others than to see it in myself?

4. What are the effects or results of sin?

- **QS** **Isaiah 59:2** What two things does sin or iniquity cause?

- **QS** **Romans 6:23** What is the payment we owe for our sin?

5. Sin causes separation and death. What is separated and what dies?
   God is a three-part God: Father, Son, and Holy Spirit. We were created in His image.

- **1 Thessalonians 5:23** What are the three parts of man?

Sin causes separation and death in all three areas:
Body, Soul, and Spirit.

1. **Our Body:** We fear physical death. Our brain, heart, and all bodily functions cease, and our soul and spirit separate from our body.

- **Genesis 2:16–17** What did God say rebellion (going my own way) causes?

- **Hebrews 9:27** What follows physical death?

2. **Our Spirit:** Sin causes a death far worse than physical death—spiritual death. God is Spirit (John 4.24). Sin causes our spirit to die, which separates us from God. Because we all sin, we all are born dead to God or separated from Him.

- **QS** Ephesians 2:1 Why does God say we are spiritually dead?

- **QS** Ephesians 2:2–3 How do those who are spiritually dead live?

- **QS** Ephesians 2:4–7 What is the answer?

- **QS** Ephesians 2:8–9 Can I earn spiritual life by my good works?

3. **Our Soul:** Our mind, emotions, and will are also affected by sin. Every sin causes something within us to die:

   Mind: Our purity of thought dies.
   Emotions: Our freedom from guilt dies.
   Will: Our desire to resist sin dies.

6. Sin kills and ruins all relationships.

   Within Us: Guilt and shame cause our self-respect to die.
   With Others: Respect, love, and trust die—separating us from loved ones.
   With God: Our spirit dies—separating us from God.

7. Forgiveness brings life and heals all relationships.
    Sin causes separation and death, but forgiveness brings unity and life. *Forgiveness* in Greek means "to send away." Sin separates but forgiveness separates (sends away) the sin from the sinner.

    *   **QS** **Ephesians 1:7** What does Jesus' blood do for you?

    *   **QS** **Ephesians 4:32** What are you then to do?

    *   **QS** **Psalms 103:3, 12** When God forgives how does He send away your sin?

    *   **Isaiah 38:17** Where does God put your sins?

    God puts your sin behind His back, which literally means "between His shoulder blades." One summer day, I wore a sundress and sat in a wicker chair. Bob asked, "How did you get those marks on your back?" As hard as I tried I could not see those marks. You cannot see between your shoulder blades! God is saying He removes our sin so you can't see it, then He puts it between His shoulder blades so He won't see it! Your sin is forgiven—sent away.

    *   Have you forgiven yourself?

Insight Day 2

When we look at others, we see our differences, but God sees our similarities. We have all sinned!

Sin is rebellion—going my way instead of God's way; doing things I should not do and not doing the things I should.

Sin affects all our relationships, but so does forgiveness. Whose sins do you need to forgive or send away?

DAY 3—Steps to Sin

1. Why do we all sin?

    Because sin has such devastating effects on our lives and relationships, we need to better understand how and why we rebel against God's way.

    - **QS** **Jeremiah 17:9** Why do we sin?

2. How important is my heart/mind?

    In the Bible, the words "heart" and "mind" are synonymous—but what does my mind have to do with sin?

    - **Matthew 15:18–19** What comes from your heart/mind? Make a list.

    - **Proverbs 4:23** What are you to do with your heart/mind?

    God says we are to keep or guard our hearts/minds because our thoughts, our words, and deeds originate there.

    - What specifically can you do to guard your mind?

    - **Proverbs 23:7** Why is guarding our thoughts so important?

3. Is sin a process?

- **Genesis 3:6** What were the steps to Eve's sin? (Note the verbs!)

- **Genesis 3:6** Did her sin affect her alone? What did she do after she ate?

- **Genesis 3:7–13, 16–19** What all was separated or died as a result of their sin?

4. Sin's Steps

- **James 1:13–15** Does God tempt us? What are the steps to your sin?

  a. Sin begins with the **eyes** . . . we are tempted by what we see and want.
  b. It leads to the **mind** . . . we consider, desire, lust after, justify, or rationalize.
  c. Our **emotions** . . . are entrapped by the desire.
  d. Our **will** acts . . . and death and separation come.

Therefore, we cannot separate our thoughts from our behavior.

IMPORTANT THOUGHT Sin is not just what we do but what we think, because what we think determines what we do.

- **Matthew 5:28** Can our seeing and thinking be sin? ("Look" is a present participle in the Greek, which expresses continuous action.)

Temptation is not sin, but what we do with that tempting thought can be.

5. Sin's Solution

  - **QS** **Ezekiel 36:25–26** What does God want to do with your sinful heart/mind?

  - **I Corinthians 2:16** Whose mind will you then have?

  - **2 Corinthians 10:5** What are you to do with your thoughts?

  - **Hebrews 10:16** When God gives you a new mind, where is God's law written?

  - **Hebrews 10:17** When He gives you a new mind what else is true?

  - If you knew your sins were forgiven and forgotten, and you had God's law written in your mind instead of a book, how would your thinking change?

Insight Day 3

Sin begins in the mind or heart and causes separation and death. Sin first separates us from God, but it also separates us from those we love.

The problem in our relationships is not that others are so different from us, but that we are the same—we all want our own way. God's solution is to give us a new heart or mind—His!

DAY 4—Answers to the Sin Dilemma

1. How can I be kept from the fatal effects of sin?
   When Travis was little and a commercial for a scary movie or undesirable program was shown on TV, he would attempt to guard his mind by closing his eyes, covering his ears, and humming a tune! As much as we adults try to do right, we don't always. For example, God says "don't worry about anything," but we all worry—therefore, we all sin!
   How can we be kept from the effects of sin? Record insights.

   • QS **Romans 6:23**

   • QS **Romans 3:28**

   We are justified by faith apart from keeping the law. The word "justified" means *just as if I'd never sinned.* Only by faith can I be made just as if I'd never sinned.

2. So what is faith?
   If faith is the only thing that will make me right with God, it is important to know what faith is. We can better understand faith by the acronym HBO'S

FAITH IS . . .		
Romans 10:17	**HEARING**	What do we need to hear to have faith?
Romans 4:20–21	**BELIEVING**	What do we need to believe to have faith?
Hebrews 11:8	**OBEYING**	When should we obey in faith?
Hebrews 11:18	**without SEEING**	Must we understand it all before obeying?

Faith is hearing the Word, believing and obeying it, without seeing the end result. D. L. Moody said, "I prayed for faith and thought someday faith would come down and strike me like lightning, but faith did not come. One day I read Romans 10:17, 'Faith comes by hearing . . . the Word of God.' I had closed my Bible and prayed for faith. Now I opened my Bible, began to study, and faith has been growing ever since!"

Insight Day 4

Faith in Jesus Christ is the only answer to my sin problem. I must:
  Hear—He loves me and died for my sin.
  Believe—adhere to, trust in, and rely on Him so that I will
  Obey—whatever He tells me even
  without Seeing or understanding it all.

"Without faith it is impossible to please God!" Hebrews 11:6

DAY 5—God's Insights Lead to New Beginnings

Rather than admit we sin, we often rationalize. Divide the word "rationalize" and you have "rational lies." We condone wrong behavior through rational lies. We excuse our impatience, explain away our anger, and justify our sarcasm often by pointing to the faults of others.

When Travis was young, he rationalized when asked if he had spilled his milk. He'd say no, it was somebody else's fault. The problem was that he was an only child, and we didn't even have a dog to blame! Adam and Eve also rationalized. When asked if they had sinned, Eve said that the devil made her do it. Adam said, "It was the woman you gave me." In other words, they blamed the devil, each other, and God!

In reality, we each have a sin problem and need a Savior. The Savior's name is Jesus. Blaming others or trying to change them to be perfect like me will not solve the problem.

1. New Insights
   a. What did you learn about Phlegmatics this week?

Phlegmatics are so nice they sometimes deceive themselves into thinking they don't need God! However, selfishness can be quiet, and the heart may not be as pure as the exterior appears.

As a child, my husband, Bob, looked sweet and obedient. He was hospitalized at age seven for a ruptured appendix. Like any Phlegmatic, he wanted peace and comfort. When a whining sick roommate disturbed the quiet, Bob quietly punched him. The nurses couldn't understand his roommate's black eye and distress because Bob looked so angelic. Phlegmatics need to see their hearts.

the amazing temperaments

b. What insights did you receive about sin this week?

c. Using God's definition of sin, can you identify any sin in your own life?

Remember, sin is:
   Rebellion against God
   Seeking the world's advice but not God's
   Going my own way instead of God's way
   Not believing His Word
   Not obeying His Word
   Not doing the good I know I should
   Breaking the law

d. How does sin affect your relationships?

IMPORTANT THOUGHT Remember, a good relationship is made up of two good forgivers!

e. How can we deal with sin?

f. What insights did you receive about faith this week?

g. Corrie Ten Boom defined faith as **F**antastic **A**dventure **I**n **T**rusting **H**im!

• **Romans 10:17** How does your faith grow?

Just as sin is a process, faith also is a process. Faith grows step by step. As you read and obey the Word, your faith and trust grow, and life becomes fantastic!

2. New Beginnings Start with God's Word
   MEMORIZE Romans 6:23

   *"For the wages of sin is death, but the free gift of God
   is eternal life in Christ Jesus our Lord." Romans 6:23*

3. New Beginnings Take Action
   a. To make right choices, we need to see where we tend to go wrong. Take a few minutes to go back over the weaknesses of each temperament listed on pages 11–12.

   - Circle those weaknesses that apply to you.

   b. Talk to God in prayer:

   1. Confess these weaknesses to God as the areas in which you will sin.
   2. Thank God for revealing them to you.
   3. Ask God to use these weaknesses to make you more like Himself.

   c. Listen to God speak:

   Hearing God requires daily Bible reading. What will you do when this study is over? There are excellent helps such as *The Daily Walk* that leads you through the Bible in a year, *The Daily Bread*, or other devotional guides. Also, there are wonderful Bible studies through such ministries as Precept Ministries or Bible Study Fellowship. As you meet with God in His Word, He will change your mind so that you will make right choices with good consequences.

   Reap right by sowing right!

 Insight Day 5 — Our weaknesses are like red flags warning us where we will be tempted to go our own way and sin. Identifying our weaknesses helps us see our need for Jesus, because He is the only one who can deal with them. He will use our weaknesses, trials, and failures to make us more like Himself.

Week FOUR

seek to go God's way

Most relationships today struggle in the area of communication. Real communication requires three things: talking, listening, and coming to an understanding or meeting of the minds. Each temperament has a different problem communicating. The Sanguine and the Choleric are good talkers, but they may need to learn to listen. The Phlegmatic and the Melancholy are good listeners, but they may need to learn to talk. Nevertheless, unless we come to an agreement or an understanding, there is not real communication!

When Travis was three years old, he was afraid of loud noises. During one severe thunderstorm, I told him not to be afraid because the thunder was just God talking. After one resounding crash, Travis pushed back the sliding door, looked into the sky and said, "God would you mind talking a little softer? You're hurting my ears!"

We, too, have fears and often wish God would communicate with us by speaking as loud as thunder. This week, we will study two Melancholies who needed to seek God's way and hear God speak to relieve their fears and find joy.

DAY 1—Meet the Melancholy

Life to a Melancholy is very serious and their motto says it all: if it is worth doing, do it right!

1. Meet Melancholy Ruth
    There was a famine in the land. Naomi, a follower of Almighty

God, went with her husband and two sons to a foreign land for food instead of trusting God to provide. While there, her sons married pagan women, Orpah and Ruth. Soon both sons and their father died. The widowed Naomi decided to go back to her homeland and to her God.

- **Ruth 1:8–17** Although both daughters-in-law had the same experience, what different choice did they make? (This is the last mention of Orpah.)

- **Ruth 1:16–17; 2:11–12** What were they choosing besides where to live?

These women were choosing whom they would worship and trust—their pagan gods or the one, true, living God. Ruth made the right choice with good consequences.

In relationships, Melancholies are very loyal, faithful, and self-sacrificing. In performing tasks, they are very conscientious, precise, and detailed.

- **Ruth 3:5** How was Ruth conscientious?

- **Ruth 4:10–13; 17; Matthew 1:1, 5** How was Ruth blessed for her right choices?

2. Meet Melancholy Moses
   Moses wrote the first books of the Bible. Acts 7:22 says he was learned in all the wisdom of the Egyptians and was mighty in words and deeds. Melancholies are gifted perfectionists, and whatever they do, they do well. They are careful and cautious, and they greatly fear making a mistake. Therefore, they are uncomfortable with deadlines because they need time to think things through, gather all the equipment, and do everything just right.

   Melancholies are distressed by imperfections and can be critical of things, others, and themselves. They are deep thinkers who must resist negative thinking. In spite of their gifts and abilities, they often struggle with insecurity and lack of self-confidence.

- **Exodus 3:7–11** What was Melancholy Moses' first response when told by God that he had been chosen to deliver Israel?

- **Exodus 3:12** What was God's answer?

- **Exodus 3:13–15; 4:1** Even though God tried to relieve Moses' fears by promising to be with him, what else did Moses fear?

- **Exodus 4:2–8** What did God do to assure negative Moses?

In spite of such a powerful display by God, Moses analyzed the situation and concluded there was another reason God had made a mistake in choosing him.

- **Exodus 4:10** Why did Moses think he was the wrong man for the job?

- **Exodus 4:11** Who made Moses' weaknesses as well as his strengths?

Melancholies analyze everything and think of all the reasons something won't work. Their ability to see everything that could go wrong drives the optimistic temperaments crazy, but it also makes Melancholies excellent engineers, doctors, architects, and scientists.

- **Romans 15:13** With what does God want us to be filled?

God wants us to have hope, joy, and peace. These characteristics are not natural for Melancholies. They need to develop a heart of praise or an attitude of gratitude to keep them focused on the positive. More than that, they need faith or trust in God so they will surrender their wills and ways to Him. Only then will the Holy Spirit produce joy and peace in them.

We can't have fear and faith at the same time. They are opposites!

Insight Day 1

We need to choose to go God's way, but even when God clearly tells us what His way is, we often fear doing it. Like Moses, we need assurance.

We need to follow Someone Who *is* the Way, not someone who just shows the way. We need to follow Someone Who *is* the Truth, not someone who just knows some truth.

DAY 2—Communicating with God

I have learned much about communicating with God through Travis. When he was five years old, we had a drippy faucet. Bob worked for hours to no avail when Travis asked, "Dad, have you prayed about it?" Of course, we hadn't prayed about it—you save prayer for the "biggies!" Travis said, "Dear Lord, please help Daddy fix the faucet." In less than a minute, the drip stopped. God says, "We have not, because we ask not." (James 4:2)

I was learning to talk to God

That same year I learned another lesson through Travis. We were in a carpool with another five-year-old and her mother. This Choleric child was being a perfect example of a sinner. She said to her mother what we say to God, "I'll do what I want to do." Her mother rolled her eyes and said, "This has been quite a day. I already had to spank her once." Travis was seated in the back seat beside the Choleric child, and he sweetly leaned over with his chin in his hands and said, "Children, obey your parents in all things, for this is pleasing to the Lord." Little Miss Choleric was not impressed, but I was. My Bible was collecting dust on my dresser while Travis was letting God speak through his.

I was learning to let God talk back

1. Why do I need to go God's way?

   • **QS** **Proverbs 14:12** What is the danger in going the way that seems right to me?

- **QS** **Proverbs 16:7** What is the great benefit to my relationships if I go God's way?

- **QS** **Proverbs 3:5–6** What does God say I should do to know His ways?

  1.

  2.

  3.

  4. What will God do?

- **QS** **Isaiah 55:8–9** What do we learn about God's way versus our way?

- **Isaiah 30:21** How does God say He will tell us His way?

2. How can I know what God's way is?
   God said, "to acknowledge Him in all our ways, and He will make your paths straight." Isaiah 30:21 tells us we will hear a voice behind us say, "This is the way, walk in it." (I hear a voice saying, "Buy diamonds!" but I don't think it is God's voice!) The world is full of voices. How can we discern God's voice?

   - **James 1:5–6** What must we do first in order to know God's way? What will God do?

The first reason to pray is to seek wisdom, but there are other reasons. Why we should pray? Record insights from the following Scriptures:

- **QS** **1 Samuel 12:23**

- **Luke 22:46**

- **John 14:13** What does prayer do for God?

- **John 16:24** What does prayer do for us?

- **QS** **Philippians 4:6–7** For what and how should we pray?

- **QS** **1 Thessalonians 5:17** When should we pray?

Worry is like a rocking chair . . . we go back and forth but don't get anyplace! Because we worry about everything, we need to pray about everything, big and small. We are to pray without ceasing—like having an incessant cough. In other words, we are to live in a daily personal relationship with God having an on-going, two-way conversation with Him. This is how to understand His mind. We talk with Him, and we give Him opportunity to talk back!

Insight Day 2 It is dangerous to make choices based on what seems right to man, because those choices may end in death. The safe choice is based on trusting the Lord and letting Him direct all our ways. The trick is to hear His voice so that we will know His way.

DAY 3—Communicating Problems

Each of the temperaments has a hard time communicating;

SANGUINES talk while you are talking . . .
or they are thinking what to say when you finish.

CHOLERICS talk at you . . .
They tell you what you think and how you feel. They don't listen.

PHLEGMATICS talk like you . . .
to avoid conflict, they agree even when they don't agree.

MELANCHOLIES are silent . . .
They analyze what you say, what you don't say, the tone of your voice, inflection, and body language. They think instead of speak.

1. What hinders my prayers, my communication with God?
    When we pray we may feel our prayers are bouncing off the ceiling. What keeps God from hearing your prayers? Record insights below.

    • **QS Psalms 66:18**

    • **Isaiah 59:2**

    • **QS James 4:2–3**

    • **I Peter 3:7**

2. If I listen, how does God speak?

There is a story of a dangerous, rocky, New England seashore that has four lighthouses. In order for a ship to land safely on shore, a ship captain must line up all four lighthouses so only one light can be seen. Only then is it safe to proceed.

I believe God speaks in four different ways just like those lighthouses. All four ways line up to reveal His perfect will. The lighthouses that help us discern what God is saying to us can be remembered by the acronym **BOSC**, like the pear: **B**ible, **O**thers, **S**pirit, **C**ircumstances.

BIBLE: God speaks through His Word, the Bible

- **QS** **Psalms 119:105** What does God's Word do?

- **QS** **Psalms 119:9–11** What else does God's Word do?

- **QS** **Psalms 119:9–11** What must we do with God's Word besides hear it?

- **2 Timothy 3:16–17** Where did the Bible come from? What does it do?

Summarize what you have learned about God's Word.

God will speak through His Word and tell you what to believe, correct what you are believing wrongly, correct what you are doing wrong, and tell you what to do right. The Bible keeps us from sin as we read, memorize, and obey it.

OTHERS: God speaks through other people

Jehoshaphat, King of Judah, was surrounded by three different enemies who came to do battle against him. Understandably, Jehoshaphat was very fearful.

- **2 Chronicles 20:3–4** What did Jehoshaphat do?

- **2 Chronicles 20:5–13** What impresses you about Jehoshaphat's prayer?

God may speak in response to our prayers, but prayer isn't just asking for help. Jehoshaphat first thought about how big His God was (20:6–9), not how big his problem was (20:10–12). He praised and thanked God before making requests.

Well-rounded prayer is remembered by the acronym CATS:

Confession—so God can hear our prayers.
Adoration—focusing on how big is our God.
Thanksgiving—remembering His past dealings and character.
Supplication (requests)—for yourself and others.

- **2 Chronicles 20:12** Was Jehoshaphat's prayer telling God what to do, or asking God what to do?

- **2 Chronicles 20:14–15** When God answers, through whom does He speak?

- **2 Chronicles 20:15** What was God's answer? What is God saying to you regarding the fears you face?

Summarize your insights on God's speaking to us through others.

God will speak through others, but what they say must line up with the plumb line of the Word of God.

SPIRIT: God speaks through His Holy Spirit

• **QS** **1 Corinthians 6:19–20** Where does God the Spirit want to be in relation to you?

• **QS** **Acts 8:29** By His Spirit, God told Philip what to do. Was it specific?

• **QS** **Acts 16:6–7** What does God's Spirit tell us besides what to do?

• **1 Kings 19:11–12** How does God's Spirit speak?

Summarize your insights on God's speaking through His Spirit.

The Holy Spirit within us speaks in a still, small voice. God speaks through our thoughts, but these thoughts must always line up with God's Word. He also speaks through inner peace or unrest. The Spirit will tell us what to do and what not to do. We must learn to recognize God's voice and obey it.

the amazing temperaments

CIRCUMSTANCES: God speaks through circumstances

God opens or closes doors of opportunity in our lives. For example, God planned to make Joseph's family a great nation. He took this young shepherd boy from the fields of Canaan and made him second in authority in Egypt. Note how God used circumstances to communicate His plan.

- **Genesis 37:23–28** What circumstance did God use to take Joseph to Egypt?

- **Genesis 41:14–16, 25–28, 38–41** What did God use to elevate Joseph to ruler?

- **Genesis 45:3–8** Did Joseph recognize God was at work in his circumstances?

Summarize your insights on circumstances.

What we see as luck, or lack of it, may actually be God directing our circumstances in order to communicate His will. He will open and close doors. We need to walk through open ones and thank Him for closed ones—not trying to break them down. Closed doors are good because they tell us what God doesn't want.

Insight Day 3

God has a plan for our lives, which He communicates to us if we ask/pray for wisdom. He will speak to us through the *Bible*, through *Other people*, through the still, small voice of His *Holy Spirit* in our heart or mind, and through our *Circumstances*. His Spirit will tell us what to do and what not to do. We must make sure every voice lines up with the Truth—God's Word, the Bible.

DAY 4—Ways God Answers Prayer

Sanguines and Cholerics are quick to speak. They tell you things you don't want to hear. Phlegmatics and Melancholies are quick to be silent. They have good answers; they just don't tell you what they are.

If you are quiet:

SANGUINES think your feelings are hurt because the only time they are quiet is when their feelings are hurt.
CHOLERICS think you must be dumb. You must not have anything intelligent to say.
PHLEGMATICS think you must be smart—because you can't improve upon silence.
MELANCHOLIES think you must be thinking—because that's what they always do.

1. Does God always answer prayer?
   Think of it! God desires a close personal relationship with you. To be sure you are hearing God's voice, you must line up the four lighthouses: The Bible, Others, the Spirit, and Circumstances. How does God answer?

   A. God's answer may be: **An Immediate Yes**

   • **QS** **Matthew 14:25–33** What was Peter's prayer (v. 30)? How was it answered?

   B. God's answer may be: **A Delayed Yes—or Wait**

   • **QS** **John 11:3–6** Did Jesus answer this prayer immediately?

   C. God's answer may be: **Different from What We Expect**

   • **QS** **John 11:3, 21** How did Mary and Martha expect Jesus to answer their request?

- **QS** **John 11:4-6, 41–44** How did God answer instead?

- **QS** **John 11:40, 45** What did God's answer do?

- **Isaiah 55:8–9** Whose way is better: ours or God's?

D. God's answer may be: **No—but He Gives Us Peace to Accept It**

- **QS** **2 Corinthians 12:7–10** Did God answer Paul's request? Did Paul have peace?

2. How can I deal with God's "no" or different answers?
- **Psalms 84:11** What does God promise?

- **Jeremiah 5:25** If good things are being withheld, what may be the problem?

- **QS** **Romans 8:28** What can we know about all that happens to us?

- **Romans 8:29** What is the good God promises to bring?

 God always answers our prayers but not always in the way we ask. Nevertheless, His answers can be trusted, because He knows what is best. His ways are higher than our ways.

DAY 5—God's Insights Lead to New Beginnings

1. New Insights
   a. What did you learn about Melancholies this week?

   b. What did you learn about communicating?

   c. What did you learn about prayer?

   d. What did you learn about how to know God's will?

   e. What did you learn about how God answers prayers?

2. New Beginnings Start with God's Word
   MEMORIZE Proverbs 3:5–6

   "Trust in the Lord with all your heart And do not lean on your own understanding. In all your ways acknowledge Him, and He shall direct your paths." Proverbs 3:5–6

3. New Beginnings Take Action

Jesus is God who has come in the flesh because He wants to have a relationship with you! Now that you have been introduced to Jesus, are you willing to learn to communicate with Him? It is as easy as ABC:

Admit—I am a sinner in need of a Savior and Lord each day.
Believe—God will speak if I will listen to His Word, Others, and His Spirit.
Choose—today to follow the risen Jesus wherever His lighthouses lead.

Insight Day 5

We must bow our knee to Jesus to know God's will for our lives. Get on your knees right now (or at least bow your heart) and turn what you have learned this week into a prayer . . . listening as much as you speak.

Week FIVE

turn from your way by being filled with the Holy Spirit

Do you remember your first bicycle? Mine was a blue Roadmaster! Just sitting on that shiny two-wheeler brought visions of speed and freedom to travel to exotic places unknown (or at least to the next block)! But do you remember learning how to ride that bike?

Actually riding, as opposed to sitting, called for such skills as keeping balance, knowing when and how to brake, recognizing hazardous conditions and so on. Often our first attempt at riding was misnamed because we couldn't even get on the bike, let alone ride it. We needed someone to run alongside to keep us from falling.

As we look at the different temperaments in the Bible, we see they needed help learning how to pedal through life. We, too, need help in finding the proper balance in day-to-day living, in learning when to stop or brake, and in recognizing dangers along the way. God realizes we need someone to come alongside and keep us from falling. Therefore, God sent the Helper—the Holy Spirit—who not only shows us the way but empowers us to follow it.

This week we will discover the answers to these questions: Who is the Holy Spirit? How does the Spirit change the weaknesses of the four temperament types? How can we be changed, too?

DAY 1—Meet the Holy Spirit

1. Who is the Holy Spirit?
    We have seen that Jesus is God with us expressing the Father's love to us by giving grace or favor we don't deserve. Who is the Holy Spirit? Record insights:

    * **Matthew 28:19**

- **QS** Acts 5:3–4

- **2 Corinthians 3:17** (What frees us?)

- **2 Corinthians 13:14**

- **Hebrews 9:14**

- **Psalms 139:7–10**

- **Isaiah 11:2**

2. How can a person relate to a spirit?
   Record personal qualities attributed to the Holy Spirit.

   - **QS** **John 16:13** What pronoun is used?

   - **Ephesians 4:30** Can He feel?

- **Revelation 2:7** Can He speak?

Summarize what you have learned about the Holy Spirit.

Insight Day 1

The Holy Spirit is God. He is called Lord. Like Jesus, the Holy Spirit has the same qualities as the Father. He is eternal, omnipresent, and wise. His role is to bring us into personal fellowship with the Father, the Son, and with each other. He brings God's wisdom and strength to our lives.

DAY 2—The Work of the Holy Spirit

1. What are the Holy Spirit's names?
    The Holy Spirit is a person to whom we can relate. He grieves and He speaks. Record what the following Scriptures say in answer to these questions: What is the Holy Spirit called? What will He do for you?

    - **QS** **John 14:26**

    - **QS** **John 16:7–11** (*Reprove* or *convict* means "to convince or tell a fault.")

    - **QS** **John 16:13** (Who is truth besides the Word and Jesus?)

    - **2 Corinthians 3:17–18**

2. What does the Holy Spirit do?
    He is our comforter and our discomforter! He teaches truth and convicts of untruth.
    What other things will the Spirit do for you?

    *   **QS John 3:3–7**

    *   **Acts 1:8**

    *   **Romans 8:26–27**

    *   **Romans 8:14–17**

    *   **1 Corinthians 2:9–13**

    *   **1 Corinthians 12:1, 4–7** What does the Spirit give each believer?

3. Where does the Spirit live?
    God the Father is on His throne; Jesus the Son is at His right hand. Where is the Spirit?
    What is He doing there?

    *   **Ezekiel 36:25–27**

- **QS** John 14:16–17

- **QS** Ephesians 1:12–14

What does it mean to be sealed with the Holy Spirit?

A SEAL:

1. **Denotes authenticity**—shows our salvation is the real thing.
2. **Identifies the owner**—like a brand signifying we belong to God.
3. **Guarantees against tampering**—nothing can separate us from God's love or take away the forgiveness and eternal life He has given us.

The Spirit enables God to live in me. Jesus is God in a body. The Holy Spirit is God living in my body. He will comfort, teach, lead, and empower me from the inside out. Because I am sealed with the Spirit (Ephesians 1:13), I know He will never leave nor forsake me (Hebrews 13:5).

Insight Day 2

As Jesus is God come in the flesh, the Holy Spirit is God come to indwell my flesh. The Holy Spirit takes up residence in those who have committed their lives to Jesus Christ as Savior and Lord.

Because He is a person with intelligence, emotions, and the ability to communicate, we can have a personal relationship with God.

DAY 3—Filled With God's Spirit

1. What does the Holy Spirit want to do besides seal me?

   - **QS** Ephesians 5:18

Just as a person filled with wine is controlled by wine, the person filled with the Spirit is controlled by the Spirit. When He controls me, the Spirit changes me and leads me into a close relationship with God Himself. When He controls me, my thoughts, words, and deeds will reflect the character of Almighty God.

2. How can I be filled with the Holy Spirit?

It is natural to be filled with myself and controlled by the strengths and weaknesses of my temperament. But what must I do to be filled with the Spirit or controlled by God? Record insights below.

- **Luke 11:13**

- **Romans 12:1–2**

- **1 Corinthians 6:19–20**

- **QS Galatians 5:16**

- **QS Galatians 5:18**

- **QS Galatians 5:24–25**

- **Colossians 3:1–2**

Being filled with the Holy Spirit depends on moment-by-moment choices I make regarding who is allowed to control my life. Am I allowing the Spirit to lead me? Have I given Him my body and my mind? Is my mind set on things above or on things of the earth?

Insight
Day 3

If the Holy Spirit is in control of my life, it will be obvious, because He alone can give:
- joy in suffering,
- love in rejection,
- peace in stress,
- patience in crises.

These are not natural responses. They are supernaturally produced by the Holy Spirit.

DAY 4—Spirit-Filled Temperaments: Up Close and Personal!

1. Meet Spirit-filled and changed Sanguine Peter.
   In Week 1, we saw that Sanguine Peter had good intentions but did not have the discipline to follow through with his intentions. After claiming He would never deny Jesus but that he would die with Him, Peter denied Jesus three times. However, God says if we walk in the Spirit, we won't fulfill the desire of the flesh (Galatians 5:16).

   a. Sanguines speak persuasively but, because they seek approval, they often say what they think others want to hear. However, Peter was changed when he followed Christ and allowed God's Spirit to fill Him and control his tongue.

   - **QS** Acts 4:8 What happened before Peter spoke?

   - **QS** Acts 4:9–12 What is Peter's message about Jesus?

   - **QS** Acts 4:13–20 Filled with the Holy Spirit, is Peter more concerned about pleasing people or presenting truth?

   b. Sanguines are positive people who see the bright side of things. However, they are greatly affected by their environment. If the people around them or their circumstances aren't fun, they often replace the people or run from the circumstances. They quit school, get divorced, change jobs, drink, etc.

- **Acts 5:18, 29–32, 40–42** What change did the Holy Spirit make in the source of Peter's joy? Were his circumstances fun?

We see new discipline in Peter. Taking an unpopular stand is difficult for people-pleasers who want to be accepted and liked. Sanguines often become like those they are with. The good news is: if they spend time with Jesus, they become like Him.

2. Meet Spirit-filled and changed Choleric Paul.

a. In Week 2, we saw Paul the prisoner telling the soldiers what to do. Cholerics lead even when they don't know where they are going. They need to learn that God must lead because He is the only one who knows all things. In order for Paul to learn this, God put him in situations where everything was out of his control.

- **Acts 9:1–4, 8–9** What did God do to get Saul/Paul's attention?

- **Acts 9:4–6** Was Paul, the Choleric leader, willing to let God lead?

- **Acts 9:10–11** What did Paul do for three days?

- **Acts 9:17–20** Did Paul receive only physical sight, or was it spiritual as well?

b. Paul was spiritually blind, but now he could see who Jesus is. For three days, Paul waited and prayed, which is contrary to the active nature of the Choleric. His *conduct* is evidence that the Holy Spirit was filling and changing him. However, the real proof that a Choleric's *character* is changed is when he demonstrates love.

- **1 Corinthians 13:1–3** Paul wrote these words. What does he say about love?

- **1 Corinthians 13:4–8a** How does Paul define love? Make a list in each column of the chart.

LOVE IS	LOVE IS NOT

- **1 John 4:7–13** Where will you get this kind of love?

Filled with the Holy Spirit, Paul is a changed man. He is still a strong-willed, active Choleric, but he is no longer prideful, impatient, and insensitive. He has new goals and projects. He also realizes that what he says, what abilities he has, what things he possesses, or what good works he does, are worth nothing without love.

 God's Spirit doesn't change our temperament, but He does turn our weaknesses into strengths. God uses each temperament as we are filled with Him.

DAY 5—God's Insights Lead to New Beginnings

1. New Insights
   a. What new insights have you received about the Holy Spirit?

   b. What have you learned about how the Holy Spirit changes weaknesses?

   c. Who is the Holy Spirit to you today?

2. New Beginnings Start with God's Word
   MEMORIZE Galatians 5:16

   > *". . . walk by the Spirit, and you will not carry out the desire of the flesh."*

3. New Beginnings Take Action

   > *"If we live by the Spirit, let us also walk by the Spirit."*
   > *Galatians 5:25*

   • List some areas of fleshly or worldly desires you are tempted by today.

   • What specific actions can you take to walk by the Spirit so you won't fulfill these desires?

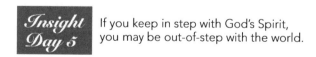 If you keep in step with God's Spirit, you may be out-of-step with the world.

the amazing temperaments

Week SIX

changed!
a new creation

When I was twenty-six years old, I trusted Jesus for "Hell Insurance." I desired to go to Heaven, and I understood that it was my sin that would keep me out. *I needed a Savior!*

As I experienced birth defects and personal conflicts, it was obvious that I needed more than Heaven someday in the future. I needed "Life Insurance" now. *I needed a Lord!*

For years, I tried New Years' resolutions to change my weaknesses or to fix my relationships, but those only lasted until January 2 in a good year! Like Peter and Paul, I needed to be changed by Someone with the power to really change me.

DAY 1—Evidence I Am Changed

1. How will I know I am filled with the Spirit?
   The Holy Spirit produces fruit in my life when conditions are right:

My life soil must be tilled—
Trials and disappointments do that.

The seed must be planted—
God's Word and Holy Spirit must be in me.

The seed must be watered and fertilized—
Bible study, prayer, and my obedience to what I know accomplishes this.

Three kinds of fruit will then be produced in my life:

1) CHARACTER FRUIT

* **Galatians 5:22–23** List the character qualities the Holy Spirit will produce in you.

* Have these qualities improved in you since Lesson One?

Do you have love, joy, peace, patience, goodness, kindness, faithfulness, humility, and self-control? It is a package deal! Jesus in you will produce all the fruit. If you lack some of these qualities, it shows conditions are not right for growth. Are you abiding and obeying?

2) CONDUCT FRUIT

* **Colossians 1:10** What kind of fruit will your conduct become?

If our conduct is not holy, God, like any good Father, may correct us.

* **Hebrews 12:11** What fruit will His correction produce?

3) CONVERT FRUIT

* **John 4:35–36** God views people as fruit ready to be harvested for what?

* **John 17:3** What is eternal life?

Because eternal life is knowing God, we don't have to wait until we die to have it. This eternal relationship with God begins the moment we receive Jesus. We know Him now and, when we die, we will know Him better—face to face.

When we know God, He wants us to see people as He does: fruitless, and also in need of eternal life. We are to sow the seed of the Word, and God will do the harvesting.

- Have you ever shared with anyone who Jesus is, what He is doing in your life, and how they can know Him, too? Why, or why not?

 The Spirit will produce the fruit of a changed character. As my character changes, my conduct will change. I will become holy and converts will be the result.

DAY 2—Why Am I Not Changed?

1. What can I become?

   - **QS** **2 Corinthians 5:17**

2. Why are many believers not filled with the Holy Spirit so they are made fruitful or new? There are at least four reasons we are not filled with God's Spirit. These four reasons can be remembered by the acronym **BLOB**:

   Bible
   Lack of Knowledge
   Obedience
   Belief

1. BIBLE:
Compare three conditions of our mind when we are filled with God's Spirit with the three results when we are filled with God's Word:

WHAT KIND OF HEART/MIND DO I HAVE WHEN I AM FILLED WITH GOD'S SPIRIT?	WHAT KIND OF HEART/MIND DO I HAVE WHEN I AM FILLED WITH GOD'S WORD?
Ephesians 5:19	Colossians 3:16
Ephesians 5:20	Colossians 3:17
Ephesians 5:21	Colossians 3:18–19

- Are the results the same or different?

- Therefore, if I want to be filled with the Holy Spirit, with what must I also be filled?

We are not filled because God's Word is of little importance to us.

2. LACK OF KNOWLEDGE:

- **Hosea 4:6a** Why are people destroyed?

We are not filled because we are ignorant of the Holy Spirit and His power. The Bible gives us knowledge of what is available to us.

3. OBEDIENCE

- **QS** **Acts 5:32** What is necessary to receive the Holy Spirit?

If we don't obey what God has given us, He won't give us more.

4. BELIEF

- **QS** **John 7:37–39** What is necessary for the Spirit to pour out of your life?

We are not filled because we don't believe (adhere to, trust in, rely on) the Holy Spirit, but we rely on our temperament strengths instead.

- How important is the Bible in your daily life?

- What specifically are you going to do to be filled with the Word so you can be filled with the Spirit?

- What is God asking you to obey so you can be filled and changed?

 Being filled with God's Spirit requires being filled with His Word and obeying it. The Bible is not merely meant to inform but to transform.

DAY 3—Spirit-Filled Temperaments: Up Close and Personal

1. Meet Spirit-filled and changed Phlegmatic Abraham.
   a. In Week Three, we saw Abraham clinging to his security. To avoid conflict, he only partially obeyed God. He took his family when God said to leave them, and he delayed going where God was taking him. He compromised to keep peace but suffered conflict instead. His dramatic transformation by God's Spirit is evident.

   - **QS** **Genesis 22:1–2** What is God doing?

   b. God tests our faith as a pilot tests a plane, not to prove it will crash, but to prove it will fly. Tests are not designed to show us we don't have faith, but to show us that we do. They also show that the One in whom we have faith is faithful.

   - **QS** **Genesis 22:3** When does Abraham obey? Does he delay?

the amazing temperaments

- **QS** **Genesis 23:3–10** How completely does Abraham obey?

- **QS** **Genesis 22:5, 8–10** In each of these verses, what tells you Abraham had faith? (Remember, faith is hearing God, believing Him, and obeying Him without seeing the result.)

- **QS** **Genesis 22:11–12** What is the consequence of total obedience?

- **QS** **Genesis 22:13–14** Was God faithful? (*Jehovah Jireh* means the Lord provides.)

- **Hebrews 11:17–19** How deep was Abraham's faith?

Phlegmatic Abraham risked conflict and even the death of his son to obey God totally—no compromise, no more delays. What an example of the power of a Spirit-controlled man!

2. Meet Spirit-filled and changed Melancholy Moses.
   a. In Week Four, we saw that Moses was a fearful man armed with many excuses as to why God couldn't use him! When God overcame his fears, Moses became a powerful leader, bringing Israel out of bondage into the freedom of the promised land.

   - **2 Timothy 1:7** What kind of spirit does the Holy Spirit not give us?

- **2 Timothy 1:7** What kind of spirit does He give us? Make a list.

b. When God told Moses He would deliver Israel through him, Moses feared he was not worthy. He feared that the people would wonder who sent him, that no one would listen to him or believe him. He feared that he wasn't eloquent or gifted enough for the task. All of Moses' fears came to pass.

- **Exodus 6:6–9** What was Israel's response to Moses' message from God?

- **Exodus 9:13–16, 34–35** What was Pharaoh's response to Moses?

- **Exodus 14:10–14** What was Moses' response to the people's fears? What is God saying about your fears?

- **Exodus 14:15–31** What was God's response? Was the God in whom Moses put his faith faithful?

- **Exodus 15:1–2** What did Moses do that kept him from getting depressed?

c. Melancholies are precise so it was to Moses that God entrusted the laws, the priesthood, and the building of the Tabernacle. He received chapters of detailed instructions on how to live and how to worship. Genesis through Deuteronomy includes volumes of details: dimensions, materials, metals, colors, fragrances, fabrics, and patterns. Only a conscientious Spirit-controlled Melancholy could have gotten it straight without going into depression over the fear of missing a cubit.

the amazing temperaments

God's Spirit gave Phlegmatic Abraham the fruit of real peace and Melancholy Moses the fruit of real joy in the midst of trials. That same Spirit desires to provide whatever real fruit you need as well.

DAY 4—Changed by Assurance

Men and women have long struggled with their self-view and relationships because they haven't answered the questions that prove their value:

Where did I come from? Why am I here? Where am I going?

1. Where did I come from?

    • **QS** **Genesis 1:26–27; 2:7** Have I evolved?

God created us in His own image, breathed His own life into us, and called us to be His own. As His children, He has a wonderful plan for each of us.

2. Why am I here?

    • **QS** **Isaiah 43:7** What is God's plan for me? Why was I created?

To give God glory means to give a correct opinion of God.

    • Does your life give a correct opinion of God to those around you?

    • **QS** **John 15:8** When do you bring God glory or give a correct opinion of Him?

It brings God glory when we thank Him for our strengths and allow Him to change our weaknesses by producing His fruit in us. Only as He changes our heart and character from the inside can we consistently give a correct opinion of God to others thus fulfilling our purpose for being.

3. Where am I going?

- **QS** **John 5:24** Of what can you be sure? Make a list.

- **2 Corinthians 5:8** Of what can you be confident when you die?

- **1 John 5:11–13** What does God want you to know? Make a list.

I can face life with great confidence and enthusiasm when I know:

Where I came from: I am a unique creation of God.

Why I am here: to give those around me a correct opinion of what God is like by allowing Him to produce His character qualities or fruit in me.

Where I am going: I know I will be absent from this body and present with the Lord because God has given me eternal life in His Son. If I have the Son, I have life. It is a sure thing.

Insight Day 4 Eternal life is knowing God—now and forever. God created me to give others a correct opinion of the God I know. I can have assurance that when I die, I will know Him even better.

DAY 5—God's Insights Lead to New Beginnings

A speaker once compared people to tubes of toothpaste. He asked the question, "When you squeeze a tube of toothpaste, what comes out?" The answer is obvious: toothpaste. He asked a second question, "When *you* are squeezed, what comes out?"

Many things may squeeze us: details, other people's weaknesses, our own weaknesses, circumstances, trials, time pressures, things, or lack of things. When you are squeezed, what comes out? The answer is: whatever is filling you. If you are full of you, your weaknesses come out. If you are full of the Holy Spirit, God's character comes out.

the amazing temperaments

IMPORTANT THOUGHT Your response to life's stresses reveals who really is in control of your life.

1. New Insights
   Think of a stress you have faced in the last few days. What came out as you were being squeezed—you and your weaknesses or God and His strengths? Why?

2. New Beginnings Start with God's Word
   MEMORIZE 2 Corinthians 5:17

   "Therefore, if anyone is in Christ, he is a new creature;
   the old things passed away; behold, new things have come."

3. New Beginnings Take Action
   To be filled with the Holy Spirit, follow these ABC's daily. Don't be a BLOB!

   Ask: the Holy Spirit through prayer to fill your heart/mind.
   Bible: read it, memorize it, study it, obey it! Let it fill you.
   Commit: choose to be led and controlled by God's Spirit. Give Him everything!
   Do: obey what you know.

4. Final Thought
   Hopefully, this study of the temperaments has given you a better understanding of your-self and others that will improve all of your relationships. However, the real answer to good relationships with others is to have a good relationship with God. Because "faith comes from hearing the Word of God," your diligence in completing this study has helped you to better know and trust God, even if you can't see the end result.

5. Trusting God Brings Abundant Life
   Jesus promised an abundant life (John 10:10), but to live abundantly I must:

   Thank God for the way I am made
   Realize others are different, and that's okay—so revise my expectations
   Understand how I will sin—or go my own way
   Seek to go God's way
   Turn from my way by being filled with the Holy Spirit

Where do you place your **TRUST**? In this life, where nothing is sure, we need to trust something that is.

Jesus is the same yesterday and today and forever.
(Hebrews 13:8)

Heaven and earth will pass away, but My words will not pass away.
(Matthew 24:35)

Jesus (and His Word): a Rock on which we can build our lives. When my father died of cancer, I saw how much freedom and assurance this unchanging truth can bring. As death approached, Dad didn't say, "I wish I had accumulated more things or I wish I had worked more hours." He was surrounded by the people he loved and who loved him, and he had assurance of where he was going. His last words were, "Haven't we had fun, and the best is yet to come!"

He was a Sanguine/Choleric!

He knew and trusted the truth about a believer's death: he would be *"absent from this body and present with the Lord."* (2 Corinthians 5:8)

I knew and trusted the truth about life's trials, including death. I could *"cast all my anxiety on Him, because He cares for"* me. (1 Peter 5:7)

6. Trusting God Brings Freedom
    1. God made me special so I don't have to try to be something I am not. I am *free* to be excited about who I am!

    2. Because we are different, I won't expect others to be like me. I will *free* them by accepting them as they are.

    3. I won't ignore or fear my weaknesses. As I ask God to deal with those weaknesses, He will *free* me from the sin that ruins relationships.

    4. I am *free* to seek God's way, but He will not force His way on me. Seeking will require communicating or developing the habit of talking and listening to God.

    5. God wants me to *free* Him to change everything about me that is not good. His Spirit will use even my weaknesses and problems to make me like Himself.

Insight Day 5

If you were born a Sanguine, you will die a Sanguine, but God wants to make you the very best Sanguine (Choleric, Phlegmatic, or Melancholy) you can be. He provides everything you need for life and godliness.

Just think how different your life would be if you had allowed God to control all your past choices! Right now, ask His forgiveness and start anew.

You are special and you are loved!

Trust God to use your strengths and to change your weaknesses. Only then can you:

Accept Yourself, Understand Others, and Like Them Anyway!

acknowledgments

Over twenty-five years ago, I read a book on the temperaments by Tim LaHaye, which started a study that changed my life. This understanding of human nature has helped in all of life's challenges—with co-workers, raising children, in marriage, with parents, etc.

Since that time, many wonderful books have been written on this topic. Although I have not referred to these books while writing this study, they are such a part of my thinking that I'm sure many thoughts from the following have been used. Even when I think an idea is original, there is "no new thing under the sun."

I don't claim any new thinking here, but I hope the truth of the temperament concept, plus my experience, along with the sure power of God's Word, will change your life as well.

Recommended reading for further study:
- *Temperament & the Christian Faith* by O. Hallesby
- *Your Temperament: Discover its Potential* by Tim LaHaye
- *Spirit-Controlled Temperament* by Tim LaHaye
- *Transformed Temperaments* by Tim LaHaye
- *Personality Plus* by Florence Littauer
- *Your Personality Tree* by Florence Littauer
- *Raising the Curtain on Raising Children* by Florence Littauer

Special thanks to my friends:
Sharon Longbottom, who started my interest in the temperaments many years ago.
Fay Runnion, who motivated me to write this study.
Ginny Miller and the **Virginia Wright Foundation**, whose love, friendship, and financial support enabled this study to be put into print.

Most of all thank you to:
The **Lord Jesus Christ**, who chooses the simple to confound the wise.
My wonderful husband **Bob Lewis** and equally wonderful son **Travis** for allowing me to use their lives as examples so we can laugh as we learn.

And . . . **YOU** for reading this far!!!

NOTES

NOTES

NOTES

NOTES

NOTES

NOTES

NOTES

NOTES

NOTES

NOTES

NOTES

NOTES

Made in the USA
San Bernardino, CA
15 May 2018